LION

by **CAROLINE ARNOLD**
photographs by **RICHARD HEWETT**
MORROW JUNIOR BOOKS • New York

PHOTO CREDITS: Permission to use the following photographs is gratefully acknowledged: Caroline Arnold, pages 26–27; Eliot Brenowicz, page 27.

The text type is 14-point Palatino.

Library of Congress Cataloging-in-Publication Data   Arnold, Caroline.   Lion / by Caroline Arnold; photographs by Richard Hewett. p. cm.   ISBN 0-688-12692-8 (trade)—ISBN 0-688-12693-6 (library)   1. Lions—Juvenile literature.   [1. Lions.]   I. Hewett, Richard, ill. II. Title. QL737.C23A754 1995 599.74'428—dc20 94-23880 CIP   AC

ACKNOWLEDGMENTS

We are extremely grateful to the staff at Wildlife Safari in Winston, Oregon, for their assistance with this project. In particular, we would like to thank Shimon Russell, senior carnivore ranger; Dr. Jack Mortenson, veterinarian; Sally Perkins, director of marketing and education; and Kassie McLellan, public relations assistant. We would also like to give special thanks to Don Jim and Eliot Brenowicz for their help. And, as always, we thank our editor, Andrea Curley, for her continuing enthusiastic support.

WHERE LIONS LIVE

A red sun rises on the eastern horizon as a mother lion gives her three-month-old cubs an early morning wash. With gentle licks, her rough tongue combs and cleans their short spotted coats. The little male lions sit still for a moment but are soon ready to play. While their mother watches quietly, the cubs tumble with each other and roll in the grass. Their soft round bodies seem awkward now, but by the time the cubs grow up, they will have the powerful, coordinated movements of adults.

The young cubs and their mother live with six other African lions at Wildlife Safari, a wild animal park in southern Oregon. The keepers know the lions well and have given each of them a name. They call the mother lion Sheeba, and her two cubs are Keno and Tsavo (pronounced SAH-vo). (Tsavo is a national park in Kenya where many wild lions live.)

The lions at Wildlife Safari occupy a large grassy area where they have plenty of room to move around. Enclosed dens provide shelter at night and when the weather is cold or rainy. The lions receive good care from the park staff and are able to live much as they would in the wild. Although the climate in Oregon is somewhat cooler than that of the lions' natural habitat, the landscape is similar in many ways to the places where wild lions live.

Most people never have the chance to see lions in the wild. Animal parks like Wildlife Safari provide an opportunity to get close to lions and learn more about them. Park staff supervise visitors as they drive through the lion enclosure and watch the animals through the closed windows of their vehicles. Although the park animals are not tame, they are used to having cars nearby and pay little attention to them.

In the wild, lions are found mainly on the grassland and open woodland of Africa south of the Sahara Desert. A few wild lions also live in India. All lions are of the same species and have the scientific name *Panthera leo.* Until ancient times, lions roamed across much of Europe. Up to the 1930s, they were found in many parts of Asia and the Middle East as well. Lions gradually disappeared in these regions as a result of hunting, climate changes, and the development of wild lands for farms and ranches.

Today, Asian lions are extremely endangered. The two hundred Asian lions that live in the Gir Forest in India are protected from hunters. They are the last of this subspecies living in the wild. African lions are not endangered, but their long-term survival is threatened by the diminishing of their natural habitat. Most African lions live in wild game preserves.

African lions.

THE CAT FAMILY

Like domestic cats, lions are members of the cat family, or felids. If you watch a lion in a wild animal park or zoo, you can see it eat, play, stretch, and sleep in many of the same ways that your pet cat does. Scientists divide the thirty-five species of felids into three groups, according to similarities in body structure. They are the big cats, the small cats, and the cheetah. Listed in order of their size, the six species of big cats are the tiger, lion, leopard, jaguar, snow leopard, and clouded leopard. The small cats include the domestic cat; bobcat; puma, which is the largest cat in this group; and twenty-five other species. One difference between the big and small cats is that the big cats can roar and the small cats cannot. The cheetah is in its own group because it is unique in many of its physical characteristics and is more distantly related to the other cat species. A fourth group of felids, the saber-toothed cats, became extinct about 10,000 years ago.

Domestic cats (above); cheetah (below).

Adult male lion (left); adult female lion (above).

Lions are the second largest of the big cats. Only the Siberian tiger, which is 12 feet (3.6 meters) long and weighs up to 700 pounds (318.2 kilograms), is bigger. A fully grown male lion is about 4 feet (1.2 meters) high at the shoulder and 9 feet (2.7 meters) long from the nose to the tip of the tail. A male lion usually weighs between 300 and 400 pounds (136.4–181.8 kilograms), but a very large one may weigh over 500 pounds (227.2 kilograms). An adult female lion, also called a *lioness*, is smaller. She is about 3 feet (.91 meter) at the shoulder and about 8 to 9 feet (2.4 to 2.7 meters) long. She weighs between 250 and 350 pounds (113.6–159.1 kilograms).

THE PRIDE

The lion is the only member of the cat family that typically lives in a large social group. (Domestic cats and tigers sometimes live in groups, but not as a rule.) The lion's social group is called a *pride.* A pride consists of one or more related females and their youngsters, which are called *cubs,* plus one or more adult males.. The pride may have as few as two adult lions in it (one male and one female) or as many as eighteen adult females and nine adult males plus a varying number of cubs. Usually there are many more females in a pride than males. The nine lions at Wildlife Safari form a single pride that includes three adult males, three adult females, and three cubs.

Lions in a pride spend most of their time together. In the wild, members of a pride often hunt together; the females share nursing and baby-sitting duties; and the cubs play with one another. When lions in a pride meet, they greet one another by rubbing their bodies together and licking one another. Unlike some other animals that live in groups, lions have no regular leader in the pride. One of the females leads the pride when it is moving to a new location, but she may take turns with other females. Usually, all members of a pride get along well together except for occasional minor squabbles.

In the wild, lion prides occupy territories that vary in size from 8 to 150 square miles (20.7 to 388.5 square kilometers), depending on how much food is available within the territory. Usually, it is the males in the pride that defend the territory from outsiders. One way that they do this is by marking the edges of the territory with urine or dung. The smell tells other lions to stay out. If a strange lion comes into a pride's territory, it will be attacked by members of the pride. Lions that live in prides have a better chance of survival. They can cooperate in finding food and caring for cubs and protect one another from other lions that might attack them.

The most noticeable difference between male and female lions is that the adult male has a thick long mane. The color of the mane varies from light yellow to brown or black. Some male lions have a mane only on the top of the head, and a few males have no manes at all; but with most lions the mane forms an elegant ruff that surrounds the animal's face and covers the head, neck, belly, and shoulders. Some male lions also have tufts of long hair on the backs of their forelegs.

Keno's and Tsavo's manes will begin to grow when they are about nine months old. A lion's mane appears first on the neck and then along the top of the head. Usually, by the time the male is five years old, his mane is thick and full. A lion's mane continues to grow throughout his life. The mane gives the male an imposing appearance and makes him look even larger than he is. The mane also helps protect the lion's neck during fights with other lions.

An adult male lion must be part of a pride in order to have the chance to mate. In most cases, females only mate with males that are part of their own pride. Adult males spend their lives either trying to take over prides dominated by other males or defending their position as the ruling males in a pride. A male lion's primary role in the pride is to mate with the females and to defend the pride against outside males. Only the strongest and healthiest males are able to maintain their rule over a pride.

In the wild, young males leave their birth pride when they are between three and four years old. Although the young males are not yet fully grown, they are able to hunt and take care of themselves. A young male lion wanders on his own or with a few other male lions. These lions without prides are called *nomads.* When the nomad lions encounter a pride, they may try to fight with the ruling adult males in it. If the nomads manage to win the fight, they will take over the pride, and the losing males will leave and become nomads. An adult male lion may stay with a pride for just a few months or for several years, depending on his ability to defend himself.

A female lion cub usually grows up and stays in the same pride all of her life. Usually, all the females in a pride are related to one another. They are mothers, daughters, sisters, aunts, and cousins. Occasionally a young female lion will leave her birth pride and join a male to start a new pride, but most prides stay together for many generations.

Lions can mate at any time of year. Both male and female lions are able to mate for the first time when they are between three and four years old. Males can tell when a female lion is ready to mate by her odor and behavior. She chooses one of the males in the pride, and they go off by themselves. They spend several days together and mate many times. After they return to the pride, they no longer show any particular interest in each other. The female may also mate with other males in the pride. After successfully mating, the female is pregnant for about three and a half months.

NEW CUBS

When it is time for her cubs to be born, a lioness finds a shady thicket or a secluded place among large rocks, where she can be alone to give birth. At Wildlife Safari, Sheeba was given her own private enclosure when it was time for her cubs to be born. Lions have been known to produce as many as seven cubs at a time, but usually a lioness has a litter of two to four furry cubs.

When Keno and Tsavo were born, they were each about 12 inches (30.8 centimeters) long and weighed between 3 and 4 pounds (1.4–1.8 kilograms). Their eyes were closed, and they could not walk or move very well. A lion cub is quite helpless during its first few weeks of life. Most of its time is spent sleeping or eating. Like other mammals, the mother lion feeds her babies milk. She lies down next to her cubs and lets them nudge their noses along her belly until each baby has found one of her four teats. Milk is the cubs' only food during their first three months, and it helps them grow quickly.

Between the ages of ten days and two weeks, the cubs' eyes open and the babies can see. By the time the cubs are six weeks old, they can walk fairly well and can follow their mother. Then it is time for the mother and her new cubs to leave their den and rejoin the pride. When several females in a pride have cubs, the mothers look after one another's youngsters and will even allow cubs that are not their own to nurse. Lion cubs continue to drink milk until they are about seven months old.

A mother lion stays with her new cubs all the time except for brief periods when she goes hunting. Lion cubs are in danger from animals such as hyenas or leopards, which might attack and kill them, so they rest quietly in their den while their mother is away. Their spotted fur helps them to hide in underbrush or in dappled shade.

A female lion with cubs does not usually mate again until her cubs are about a year and a half old. By the time the new cubs are born, her cubs from the previous litter have become part of the pride and can take care of themselves. In the wild, fewer than half the cubs grow to be adults. Many fall victim to disease, starvation, or predators. In some cases, male lions that take over a pride kill all the cubs in it. A female that loses her cubs usually mates again right away.

At Wildlife Safari, the veterinarians check the lions regularly to make sure that they are healthy. When the cubs are small, people can pick them up and handle them, but even then they must be careful of the cubs' sharp teeth and claws.

When lion cubs are about six weeks old, their first teeth appear in the front of their mouths. By the time they are nine weeks old, the cubs have full sets of baby teeth. The baby teeth fall out and are replaced by permanent teeth when the cubs are between thirteen and fifteen months old.

Lions have needle-sharp claws that make fierce weapons. Like all other cats except cheetahs, lions are able to pull in their claws when they are not using them. This protects the claws and helps to keep them sharp. Lions use their claws when hunting, fighting, and climbing trees.

Like other young animals, Keno and Tsavo were curious about their surroundings, and as soon as they could walk, they began exploring. They climbed trees, chased insects, and got to know the other lions in the pride. These kinds of activities help the cubs strengthen their muscles and become well-coordinated. As the lion cubs grew, they also developed larger appetites.

In the wild, young lions begin to accompany the pride on hunting expeditions when they are about three months old. Then, for the first time, they have the chance to eat meat.

ON THE HUNT

Lions are carnivores, or meat eaters, and hunt other animals for food. Animals that hunt and kill other animals are called predators; the animals they hunt are called prey. Lions are the top predator on the African plain. Their prey includes grass-eating animals such as zebras, giraffes, wildebeests, and species of antelope such as gazelles and impalas. Lions follow these herds of animals as they move across the plain. Lions also hunt smaller animals such as warthogs when large prey is not available. Except for elephants, hippos, and rhinos, which are large enough to defend themselves against lions, all animals are wary when a pride is near.

Like other predators, lions often prey on old or sick animals because they are easier to catch than younger animals, which can run fast enough to get away when being chased. By killing the weaker animals, lions help keep the herds strong and healthy. Lions also sometimes feed on animals killed by other predators such as leopards or cheetahs. If lions see vultures circling overhead, they know that there is a sick or dead animal nearby. Vultures are good at spotting dead or dying animals.

Gazelles in Nairobi National Park, Kenya (above); zebras in Kenya (below).

When a pride goes hunting, the females usually go first, and the males follow at a distance with the cubs. Lion cubs depend on the older lions in the pride to share food with them until they can hunt for themselves. When a cub is about two years old, it is big and strong enough to help the older lions in the pursuit of prey.

Both male and female lions hunt, but female lions are generally better hunters than males. The large mane of the male lion makes it harder for him to hide in the grass. Also, females are lighter than males, so they are faster and more agile in a chase. Most of the hunting is done by the females in the pride, and they often work together. When one lioness starts the chase, she forces the prey to run toward another lioness that is ready to make the kill. Lions that hunt together are more likely to be successful than a lion that hunts alone.

Lions usually begin their hunt in the early evening. As they walk through tall grass, they hold their tails up high. The dark tuft at the end of the tail is easy to see and helps the lions to keep track of one another.

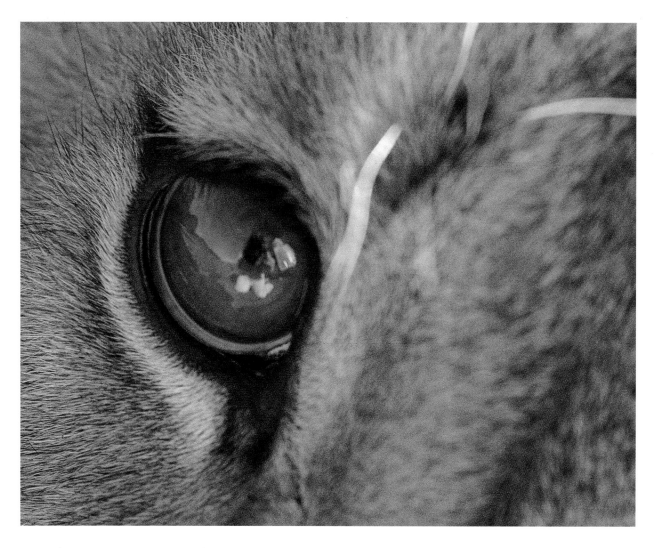

Almost every part of a lion's body helps to make it a good hunter. Lions have excellent vision and are able to spot moving objects even when they are far away. Their eyes are larger than those of any other carnivore, and, like other cats, lions can see quite well in the dark. Lions are more active at night and do most of their hunting between sunset and sunrise. When the lion hunts during the day, its tawny color is similar to that of dry grass and helps the lion to sneak up on its prey without being seen.

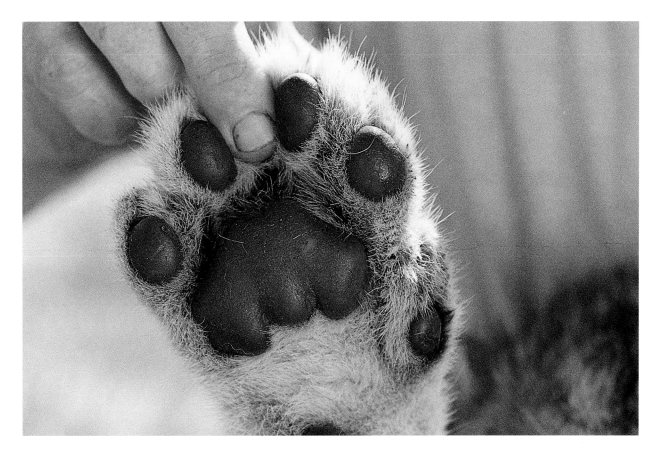

Soft pads on the bottom of the feet help a lion walk quietly, and strong legs help it chase and catch prey. Lions cannot run fast over long distances, but they can run at speeds up to 35 miles (56.5 kilometers) per hour in short spurts. When a lion reaches its prey, it uses its powerful back legs to spring forward and attack. Reaching out with one of its front paws to pull down its victim, the lion then grasps the head in its strong jaws. The lion either breaks the animal's neck or bites into the throat and strangles it.

Lions are expert hunters, but even so, they are not always successful. Lack of cover may make it hard for the lion to hide while stalking its prey. If the lion hesitates or slips in its attack, the animal may escape. Only a quarter of a lion's hunting attempts result in food to eat.

EATING AND DRINKING

Even though the lionesses are the members of the pride that usually make the kill, they and the cubs wait until the adult male or males in the pride finish eating before they begin. The females eat next, and the cubs are allowed to have whatever is left. When food is scarce, cubs often starve. At Wildlife Safari, the adult male lions are usually fed separately from the females and cubs. When they were fed together, Keno and Tsavo learned to wait patiently until the older male lions were done eating.

The adult lions at Wildlife Safari each get 10 pounds (4.6 kilograms) of fresh meat at every feeding, and the cubs get 6 to 8 pounds (2.7 to 3.6 kilo-grams) each. The keepers also give the lions vitamin and mineral supplements. (Wild lions get their vitamins and minerals by eating small pieces of bone and the stomach contents of the animals they kill.)

In the wild lions do not always eat every day, especially if they have killed a large animal and eaten a big meal. In some cases, a lion eats as much as 60 pounds (27.3 kilograms) of food at one feeding. Then it can go for several days before it is hungry again. At Wildlife Safari, the animal keepers feed the lions five out of every seven days to give them a meal schedule similar to that of lions in the wild.

A lion's strong jaws and sharp teeth are well suited to its diet of meat. An adult lion has a total of thirty teeth, sixteen in the upper jaw and fourteen in the lower jaw. The sharp incisor teeth in the front of the mouth are good for biting, and next to these are the lion's long canine teeth. These bite deeply and are used for killing prey. In lions and other meat eaters, the large teeth in the sides of the mouth are sharp and jagged. When the lion bites a piece of meat, these teeth slide against one another like the blades of scissors to cut and slice it. The molar teeth in the back of the mouth are used for crushing bones. Lions do not chew their food. Instead, they bite off chunks and swallow them whole. Strong stomach juices help them to digest their food and dissolve small pieces of bone.

Soon after a lion finishes feeding, it goes to a river or water hole to drink, using its long tongue to lap up water into its mouth. A lion can only get a small amount of water at a time, so it takes about ten minutes to satisfy its thirst. Lions may sometimes go for two or three days without water, but they need to drink regularly and usually stay close to a source of water. At the wild animal park, a small stream runs through the lion enclosure, so they can drink whenever they feel thirsty.

GROOMING

After satisfying its hunger with a good meal, a lion settles down to clean, or groom, itself with its tongue. Adult lions often lick one another's fur, and mother lions groom their cubs. The lion's rough tongue is covered with small horny spikes called *papillae*. The papillae work like a brush or comb when the lion is cleaning itself. The papillae also help the lion scrape pieces of meat off bones and lick them clean.

RESTING

When Keno, Tsavo, and the other lions get tired, they look for comfortable places to stretch out and take a nap. Lions in a pride often rest lying side by side. In some parts of Africa, lions are famous for sleeping in trees. Scientists think that they may do this to get away from bothersome insects on the ground. In most cases, however, lions sleep on the ground, often in the shade of a rock or a tree.

Like other members of the cat family, lions spend much of their lives asleep. They rest or doze seventeen hours or more each day! In this way lions save their energy for hunting.

ROARING

Male lions make loud roaring noises to let one another know where they are. They also roar to warn other lions to stay out of their territory. The low-pitched sounds of the male's roar can be heard for many miles. Lions have good hearing, and their ears can turn to catch sounds from several directions. Most roaring is done in the early evening and just before dawn. Females make softer roars to call their cubs. Lions also cough, growl, and snarl as warnings to one another. Lions purr when they are contented, although they cannot purr as well as the small cats.

GROWING UP

As Keno and Tsavo grow older, they spend more of their time playing both with each other and with the other lions in the pride. They wrestle, chase, and pounce, and sometimes give each other playful bites. A favorite activity of lion cubs is stalking the long twitching tails of the older lions. For young lions in the wild, these "games" help them practice hunting skills that are essential for their survival later in life.

Adult female lions sometimes play too, usually with the cubs in the pride. Mature male lions do not play, although a male may lie quietly while the cubs climb over him or chase his tail. When he has had enough, he lets the cubs know by giving them a swat with his large padded paw.

When a lion cub is six to eight weeks old, the dark spots it had at birth change to open rosette shapes. As the cub matures, the spots gradually grow lighter and disappear. Between the ages of three and five months, the cub's soft woolly coat gradually changes to the sleek fur of an adult. An adult lion's coat consists of short light-colored hairs next to the skin, which help keep the lion warm, and, on top of them, longer dark hairs that provide a protective outer layer.

By the time a cub is one year old, it weighs about 100 pounds (45.5 kilograms). After its permanent teeth grow in and it is able to eat more meat, it begins to gain weight rapidly. At the age of two it is about two-thirds the size of an adult; and by the time it is four years old, the lion has reached its adult length. Lions continue to gain weight until they are about six years old as their bodies become stronger and more massive.

Lions can live to be thirty years old, although even in captivity few live to be more than twenty. Wild females usually live to be fifteen to eighteen years old. Wild male lions have more stressful lives and rarely live longer than eleven years. Even though lions are top predators, life in the wild is not easy. They must compete for food with other meat eaters such as leopards, hyenas, and wild dogs. And, as people and livestock move into the places where lions live, the wild animals on which lions depend for food become harder to find.

Captive lions like Keno and Tsavo can expect to live long, healthy lives. The oldest lion at Wildlife Safari is Jasper, a fourteen-year-old male. Most zoo and wildlife park lions have never known life in the wild. Lions breed readily in zoos and wild animal parks, and, with good care, they adapt quite well to life in captivity. Special programs to breed Asian lions in zoos are helping to prevent that subspecies from becoming extinct.

THE KING OF BEASTS

People have been fascinated by lions since prehistoric times. More than 15,000 years ago, people made drawings of lions on cave walls in France. In ancient Egypt, the pharaohs took lions with them when they went into battle. Even today, in some African tribes, the killing of a lion is an important test of courage for young men. All over the world, lions have always been one of the most popular attractions in zoos and circuses.

Lions have long been a symbol of power and strength. The male lion's luxurious-looking mane and regal bearing have helped to earn it the title King of Beasts. Captive lions like Keno, Tsavo, and the other members of their pride help us to appreciate the strength and beauty of these magnificent predators. In Africa and India scientists have been studying wild lions to find out more about them and their relationship to other animals that share their natural habitat. As we learn more about lions, we can better assure a place in the wild for the most majestic of the big cats.

INDEX